TABLE OF CONTENTS

Investing Lessons
I Learned the Hard Way

Finding Security in Timeless Truths

MOODY PRESS
CHICAGO

ISBN 0-8024-3996-9

Library of Congress Cataloging in Publication Data

1 3 5 7 9 10 8 6 4 2

Printed in the United States of America

FOREWORD

I have known Austin Pryor for almost twenty years now, and I regard him as a good friend. As I have observed him over the years, I have found his counsel to be both biblical and practical. I know of no other individual with whom I would consult with more confidence on the subject of mutual fund investing than Austin.

I believe the true character of an investment adviser is not only the degree of success he has achieved, but the integrity that is maintained in the process. Austin has achieved success in the business world, but, more important, he has done so with truth and honesty.

Obviously you, the reader, must evaluate his advice yourself. No one individual has the right advice for everyone, and anyone can, and will, be wrong in the changing economy we live in. But if you will spend the time to read carefully the counsel Austin provides, you will find it both time and money well spent.

I encouraged my good friends at Moody Press to contact Austin about publishing his writing because I felt he had information that would benefit God's people. We are in no way competitors. Austin and I are collaborators in God's plan to help His people become better stewards of His resources.

Larry Burkett

The biblical principles reflected in this booklet are the foundation for the advice given in *Sound Mind Investing*, my book published by Moody Press. The material in this booklet has, for the most part, been excerpted from that book. As Christians, we acknowledge God as the owner of all. We serve as His stewards with management privileges and responsibilities. The practical application of biblical principles leads us to encourage a debt-free life-style and conservative approach to investing such as that shown in what we call the Four Levels of Investing:

Level One: Getting Debt-Free
"The rich rules over the poor, and the borrower becomes the lender's slave."
Proverbs 22:7

Paying off debts which are carrying 12%-18% per year interest charges is the best "investment" move you can make. So, get to work on paying off those credit cards, car loans, student loans, and other short-term debts. Accelerating the payments on your house mortgage, if any, should also be your goal—albeit a longer-term one. It should be your first priority to see the day when you're meeting all current living expenses, supporting the Lord's causes, and completely free of consumer debt.

Level Two: Saving for Future Needs
"There is precious treasure and oil in the dwelling of the wise, but a foolish man swallows it up." Proverbs 21:20

Even if you've not completely reached your Level One goal, it's still a good idea to set aside some money for emergencies or large purchases. A prudent rule of thumb is that your contingency fund should be equal to three to six months' living expenses. We suggest $10,000 as an amount suitable for most family situations.

Level Three: Investing in Stocks
*"Well done, good and faithful servant. You were faithful with a few things,
I will put you in charge of many things." Matthew 25:21*

Only money you have saved over and above the funds set aside in
Level Two should be considered for investing in the stock market.
In Levels One and Two, any monthly surplus was used in a manner
that *guaranteed* you would advance financially—there are no guarantees in the stock market. You should initiate a program of stock
mutual fund investing geared to your personal risk temperament
and the amount of dollars you have available to invest.

Level Four: Diversifying for Safety
*"Divide your portion to seven, or even to eight, for you do not know what
misfortune may occur on the earth." Ecclesiastes 11:2*

Once you accumulate $25,000 in your investment account, it's time
for further diversification. By adding investments to your holdings
that "march to different drummers," you can create a more efficient,
less volatile portfolio. The single most important diversification
decision is deciding how much to invest in stocks versus bonds.
That's why determining your personal investing temperament, and
following the guidelines given, can be so helpful.

Free Upon Request
Articles that guide you through the Four Levels—help on getting
debt-free, saving strategies, and updates on specific no-load mutual
fund recommendations that are geared to your personal risk tolerance—appear in my monthly newsletter, also called *Sound Mind
Investing*. In it, I offer a conservative investing strategy based on the
careful use of no-load mutual funds. For a free sample copy, simply
return the postage-paid card included at the back of this booklet.

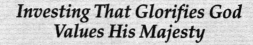

Investing That Glorifies God Values His Majesty

O God, you are my God, earnestly I seek you; my soul thirsts for you, my body longs for you, in a dry and weary land where there is no water. I have seen you in the sanctuary and beheld your power and your glory. Because your love is better than life, my lips will glorify you. I will praise you as long as I live, and in your name I will lift up my hands. My soul will be satisfied as with the richest of foods; with singing lips my mouth will praise you. On my bed I remember you; I think of you through the watches of the night. Because you are my help, I sing in the shadow of your wings.
(Psalm 63:1-7)

As in other areas of life, there is a relationship between your financial decision-making and the glory of God.

Have you ever noticed that the theme of God's glory is a continuous golden thread, which is woven throughout Scripture? We see it operative from the opening story of creation through the triumphal establishment of Christ's kingdom. The infinite worth of God's glory is emphasized over and over again. We should, therefore, be mindful that in all of our daily decision-making, including that small part that has to do with our financial and investing decisions, our primary goal must always be kept uppermost in mind—that of glorifying our wonderful God.

In this booklet, we will explore what investing "for the glory of God" might involve.

We begin by recognizing that He is sovereign and the owner of all things. Being sovereign means "possessed of supreme power that is unlimited in extent, enjoying autonomy, having undisputed ascendancy." We see this aspect of God portrayed in Scripture repeatedly.

> David praised the Lord in the presence of the whole assembly, saying, "Praise be to you, O Lord, God of our father Israel, from everlasting to everlasting. Yours, O Lord, is the greatness and the power and the glory and the majesty and the splendor, *for everything in heaven and earth is yours*. Yours, O Lord, is the kingdom; you are

exalted as head over all. Wealth and honor come from you; *you are the ruler of all things.* In your hands are strength and power to exalt and give strength to all." (1 Chronicles 29:10-12)

"Hear, O my people, and I will speak, O Israel, and I will testify against you: I am God, your God. I do not rebuke you for your sacrifices or your burnt offerings, which are ever before me. I have no need of a bull from your stall or of goats from your pens, for every animal of the forest is mine, and the cattle on a thousand hills. I know every bird in the mountains, and the creatures of the field are mine. If I were hungry I would not tell you, for *the world is mine, and all that is in it.*" (Psalm 50:7-12)

His dominion is an eternal dominion; his kingdom endures from generation to generation. All the peoples of the earth are regarded as nothing. *He does as he pleases* with the powers of heaven and the peoples of the earth. No one can hold back his hand or say to him: "What have you done?" (Daniel 4:34-35)

Amazingly, although God is sovereign over all He has made and could dictate our every thought and movement, He tolerates pockets of resistance to His reign. He allows mankind to make a decision of monumental importance: whether to willingly embrace Christ's rule in our lives and affections or to continue exercising our own self-rule and independence. We are allowed the audacity of challenging His "undisputed ascendancy" in our own lives.

What makes the choice so difficult is that the results are counterintuitive. If we should abdicate control of our lives and invite His Spirit to guide us according to His purposes, we would expect a loss of freedom, power, and happiness. *The actual result is just the opposite.* We are never more free, never have more strength to reach our potential, and never experience more fulfillment than when we acknowledge His sovereignty over our lives. The reason for this is that only when we place our faith in Christ does He come to live within us, and it is His actual presence—the personal presence of the omnipotent Creator God of the universe—that raises our daily existence to a higher, entirely new level of existence.

On the other hand, we can choose to continue living independently, doing as we think best. We expect that way of living will give us the best chance of building a future that will be the most satisfying. But again, the result is just the opposite of what we expect. We find that achieving our goals provides only short-lived fulfillment. The thrill of acquiring material possessions wears off. Fame has a short shelf-life, and perversely it creates greater anxiety than emotional security. A famous Hollywood producer, when asked how fame, fortune, and immense popularity had changed his life, gave this startling reply: "Success means never having to admit you're unhappy." His success did not end his unhappiness; it just allowed him to deny it.

The most important investing decision any person makes is this: How will we invest *ourselves*? To what purpose do we commit our lives? Followers of Christ answer by making the decision to acknowledge His sovereignty—not only over the physical universe, but over our very lives as well. This involves asking Christ to take our lives and make us the kind of people He wants us to be. We give Him our lives. God says: "If you'll give me your life, I'll give you My life." It's been called "The Great Exchange." In light of who He is and all that He offers, what could be more reasonable?

> "Who has known the mind of the Lord? Or who has been his counselor? Who has ever given to God, that God should repay him?" For from him and through him and to him are all things. To him be the glory forever! Amen. Therefore, I urge you, brothers, in view of God's mercy, to offer your bodies as living sacrifices, holy and pleasing to God—*this is your spiritual act of worship*. Do not conform any longer to the pattern of this world, but be transformed by the renewing of your mind. Then you will be able to test and approve what God's will is—his good, pleasing and perfect will. (Romans 11:34-12:2)

It should go without saying that when we present ourselves to God as "living sacrifices," our material possessions are included.

After surrendering all that we are and ever hope to be to His eternal sovereignty, the idea that we're also acknowledging God's ownership of the world's wealth (including ours) shouldn't be surprising. When we made The Great Exchange, part of the transaction involved exchanging ownership privileges for management responsibilities. It's called stewardship.

Investing means to give up the use of something now in order to have something you desire more later. The Christian gives up, surrenders, loses his earthly life now in order to receive something of far greater value later—the voice of the Lord saying, "Well done, good and faithful servant. You have been faithful over a little; I will put you over much. Enter in to the joy of your master."

What does God want from you more than anything else? It's a sobering question.

I began dealing with this early in my adult life. I knew God wanted my obedience, my service, my thanksgiving, and much more. But what did He want *the most?* I really didn't know the answer until the summer of 1973.

At the time, my wife Susie and I were on the staff of Campus Crusade for Christ, and we had traveled to Fort Collins, Colorado, for an annual event within Crusade known as "staff training." The staff had gathered together for a week of vision-building workshops and seminars. We heard many inspirational speakers, but there was one in particular who quickly captured everyone's attention. To say that Ronald Dunn's messages were well-received would be to greatly understate his impact. I have talked with Crusade staff who, 15 and 20 years later, still recall with great appreciation (as I do) how his words were so encouraging to them that summer.

I still remember, vividly, the question he posed as he set the stage for one of his primary points: "What is it, do you believe, that God wants from you more than anything else?" What would you have said? From my notes, Ron's answer went something like this:

> I believe it is the testimony of the word of God, in both the Old and New Testaments, that the primary thing, the ultimate thing, that God wants from us is not our service. *He wants our searching!* That we would seek the Lord. That we would seek the Lord.

In Acts 17, Paul leaves no doubt that *the* primary purpose behind all of God's creative work is that we would seek Him.

> "The God who made the world and everything in it is the Lord of heaven and earth and does not live in temples built by hands. And he is not served by human hands, as if he needed anything, because he himself gives all men life and breath and everything else. From one man he made every nation of men, that they should inhabit the whole earth; and he determined the times set for them and the exact places where they should live. God did this *so that men would seek him*, and perhaps reach out for him and find him, though he is not far from each one of us."

More than anything else, the Lord wants us to seek Him. He wants to be the object of our affection and the focus of our attention. He wants to draw us to seek Him. Now some may ask how the idea of "seeking the Lord" applies to Christians who have already sought Him out and placed their faith in Him. Ron's response was tremendous:

> When the apostle Paul wrote to the church at Philippi, he recounted his conversion experience, saying: "But whatever was to my profit, I now consider loss for the sake of Christ. What is more, I consider everything a loss compared to the surpassing greatness of knowing Christ."

> If I'd been writing that I might have said "the surpassing greatness of serving Christ." You know, he's had about every experience a fellow could have. There's not been anybody that has been able to serve in the magnificent magnitude that the apostle Paul has. Yet he comes to the end of this life and he says "I am continually giving up everything and counting everything but loss that I may. . . know Him."

> Well, now Paul, I thought you already knew Him. You met Him on the road to Damascus thirty or forty years ago. What do you mean you're counting everything but loss that you may know Him?

> Paul would say: "Well, you can know Him, and then you can know Him some more." You can know Him, and you can know Him, and you can know Him, and you can know Him some more. You see, my friends, the Christian life is not starting with Jesus, and then graduating to something better. It is starting with Jesus, staying with Jesus, and ending up with Jesus.

> He's the Means to the end, and He's the End. He's the Door, and He's what you find on the other side of the door. He's the Light of the world, and He's what you see when that light shines. He's the Fountain, and He's

also the Living Water that comes out of the fountain. He's the Alpha and the Omega. He's all that you need.

And so to seek the Lord means that we seek for nothing else. We find in Jesus Christ our all in all. And so Paul is saying that the quest of the Christian life is not "How can I trust Him more?" or "How can I serve Him more?" but "How can I know Him better?"

The goal of the Christian life is not service. The goal of the Christian life is Jesus. And our service is the overflow of our fellowship with the Lord Jesus Christ. So it means we need seek for nothing else, but it also means that we should settle for nothing less.

I'll tell you what I think is happening in evangelical circles today. I believe it's this: that we are settling for something less than the Lord Jesus Christ. We were on our way with Jesus, and we met something else along the way that caught our attention, and we settled for that.

I started out with the Lord. My heart was filled with the joy of the Lord. Man, I just wanted the Lord, that's all! I was seeking the Lord, but in my seeking the Lord, along the way, I found service. And I find that often I end up settling for that.

Let me encourage you in something. As you seek the Lord, if you meet service, or a gift, or a doctrine along the way, don't stop and settle for that. Please, you must keep on going and seek the Lord. Constantly seek the Lord. Don't settle for anything less than Jesus, and the fullness of fellowship with Him day by day.

As I listened to Ron, it was immediately clear to me that I had taken a wrong turn somewhere. My serving God was a well-intentioned "living sacrifice," which I desired would please Him, but it also represented a kind of detour. I so desired to serve Him, to "invest" my life for Him, *that I no longer had time to seek Him.* I resembled the workaholic husband who had little time for his wife, and when she pointed this out he claimed he was "doing it all for her."

This error can be quite a subtle thing; it seems to happen in the smallest of increments. You are not even aware of it until one day God works through your circumstances to get your undivided attention, and you "awaken" to find yourself miles off course.

Investing that glorifies God must see *Him* as the pearl of great price...

...and we joyfully sell all that we have so that we may experience the priceless treasure of fellowship with God in Christ Jesus. We value His majesty and our communion with Him above all earthly ambitions and wealth. There is no greater thrill, no greater joy than to walk away from a time of prayer and meditation *having met God.* It is as Jonathan Edwards has written:

> The enjoyment of God is the only happiness with which our souls can be satisfied. To go to heaven, fully to enjoy God, is infinitely better than the most pleasant accommodations here. . . . [These] are but shadows; but God is

the substance. These are but scattered beams; but God is the sun. These are but streams; but God is the ocean. (J. Edwards, *The Works of Jonathan Edwards* [Edinburgh: Banner of Truth Trust, 1974], p. 244.)

To glorify God, we must see Him as our great treasure. Our hearts and lives must be kept centered in Him. Christian service, although done in His name, is no substitute. Obtaining, securing, and increasing our store of wealth, although used for family support and kingdom purposes, is no substitute.

To invest more time, thought, energy, research, and emotional energy in these areas than we invest in enjoying His presence is to grieve His Father's heart. There are at least three reasons this must be true.

❶ It reveals that our pleasures are misplaced.

To delight more in the companionship of the creation around us than in the Creator who made us is idolatry. Even to delight more in the gifts we offer Him than in the gift His presence offers us is to elevate our glory above His. Our pleasure is to be in Him.

O God, you are my God, *earnestly I seek you; my soul thirsts for you, my body longs for you,* in a dry and weary land where there is no water. I have seen you in the sanctuary and beheld your power and your glory. Because your love is better than life, my lips will glorify you. I will praise you as long as I live, and in your name I will lift up my hands. My soul will be satisfied as with

the richest of foods; with singing lips my mouth will
praise you. On my bed I remember you; I think of you
through the watches of the night. Because you are my
help, I sing in the shadow of your wings. My soul clings
to you; your right hand upholds me. (Psalm 63:1-8)

❷ It reveals that our confidence is misplaced.

Isn't our security, whether spiritual, physical, emotional, or
material, to be found in His loving promises rather than our
human efforts and disciplines? Our confidence is to be in Him.

One thing I ask of the Lord, this is what I seek: that I may
dwell in the house of the Lord all the days of my life, to
gaze upon the beauty of the Lord and to seek him in his
temple. *For in the day of trouble he will keep me safe* in his
dwelling; he will hide me in the shelter of his tabernacle
and set me high upon a rock. (Psalm 27:4-5)

Keep your lives free from the love of money and be content with what you have, because God has said, "Never
will I leave you; never will I forsake you." *So we say with
confidence, "The Lord is my helper*, I will not be afraid.
What can man do to me?" (Hebrews 13:5-6)

❸ It reveals that our gratitude is misplaced.

To whom or what do we owe our successes? The free-
enterprise system that rewards hard work? The company
we labor for that gave us the chance to show what we could
do? The government programs that provided needed assis-
tance? Our investment counselor or broker who helped us
have a good year? No, God is the source of our blessings and

"the giver of every good gift." Our gratitude should be toward Him.

> David praised the Lord in the presence of the whole assembly, saying, "Praise be to you, O Lord, God of our father Israel, from everlasting to everlasting. Yours, O Lord, is the greatness and the power and the glory and the majesty and the splendor, for everything in heaven and earth is yours. Yours, O Lord, is the kingdom; you are exalted as head over all. *Wealth and honor come from you*; you are the ruler of all things. In your hands are strength and power to exalt and give strength to all. Now, our God, we give you thanks, and praise your glorious name." (1 Chronicles 29:10-13)

The kingdom of heaven, and the King who reigns over it, are "like treasure hidden in a field. When a man found it, he hid it again, and then in his joy went and sold all he had and bought that field."

Do our daily lives—the decisions we make and the dreams we pursue—reflect that Christ is our treasure?

It is my earnest hope and prayer that I would faithfully seek the majesty of His companionship daily. My practice is, however, that too often I settle for too little. Perhaps you can identify with me in this. If so, may God grant us that we increasingly glorify Him in our seeking. John Piper beautifully sums up the relationship between our desire to please

God and His desire to be glorified in our lives.

> God's deepest commitment to be glorified and my deepest longing to be satisfied are not in conflict, but in fact find simultaneous consummation in his display of and my delight in the glory of God. Therefore the goal of preaching is the glory of God reflected in the glad submission of the human heart. And the supremacy of God in preaching is secured by this fact: *The one who satisfies gets the glory; the one who gives the pleasure is the treasure.* (John Piper, *The Supremacy of God in Preaching* [Grand Rapids: Baker Book House, 1990], p. 26.) ♦

Investing That Glorifies God Builds His Kingdom

Remember this: Whoever sows sparingly will also reap sparingly, and whoever sows generously will also reap generously. Each man should give what he has decided in his heart to give, not reluctantly or under compulsion, for God loves a cheerful giver. And God is able to make all grace abound to you, so that in all things at all times, having all that you need, you will abound in every good work.... Now he who supplies seed to the sower and bread for food will also supply and increase your store of seed and will enlarge the harvest of your righteousness.
(2 Corinthians 9:6-10)

In 1848, his mother worked as a shoemaker to support the family. At the age of 13...

...Andrew went to work in a textile mill to help ease the financial burdens. He worked 12 hours a day; he was paid $1.20 a week. He decided to go to night school to learn bookkeeping so he would qualify for a better job.

The next year Andrew got a job as a messenger for a telegraph company. Wanting to advance, he returned to night school to study telegraphy. His diligence paid off with a promotion to telegraph operator two years later. He continued to improve at his work and soon became one of the few people who could "read" the sound of telegraph clicks without looking at the readout. This brought him to the attention of a railroad executive who offered him a job as his personal telegrapher and secretary. He was 17 years old and earning $8.10 a week.

Andrew continued to study as he worked, learning how railroads operated. He borrowed money to invest in the first "sleeping car" company; then, he convinced his boss to buy sleeping cars for the railroad. By the time he was 28, Andrew's earnings had risen to $1,250 a week from his salary and investment income.

In 1865, he left his job and went to Europe to sell securities in the new American railroad companies. While in England, he learned of Bessemer's new process of steelmaking. When he returned to the U.S. in 1872, he gave up his other businesses and concentrated on steel. He was eventually able to persuade railroad managers to replace iron rails with steel ones. By 1889, his mills were producing more than a half-million tons of steel per year. At the turn of the century, he employed more than twenty thousand people. His was the largest industrial concern the world had ever known. When he sold his company to J. P. Morgan in 1901, he netted more than $200 million. On that day, Andrew Carnegie became the richest man in the world.

He was fond of saying, "The man who dies rich, dies disgraced." Once he retired, he spent the rest of his life trying to give away his entire fortune, most of it for educational purposes. How different a view from today's philosophy of life, which is so forthrightly proclaimed on bumper stickers saying: "Whoever dies with the most toys wins."

What is a proper motivation for our ambition and hard work? Carnegie, although a generous man, nevertheless devoted his life to building his own kingdom. Christians follow One who is building another kind of kingdom.

> Jesus went through all the towns and villages, teaching in their synagogues, preaching the good news of the kingdom and healing every disease and sickness. . . . Then he said to his disciples, "The harvest is plentiful, but the workers are few. Ask the Lord of the harvest, therefore, to send out workers into his harvest field." (Matthew 9:35-38)

And what is the mission of these workers? Consider the final command Jesus gave to His disciples just before His ascension. It's been called "The Great Commission."

> All authority in heaven and on earth has been given to me. Therefore go and make disciples of all nations, baptizing them in the name of the Father and of the Son and of the Holy Spirit, and teaching them to obey everything I have commanded you. And surely I am with you always, to the very end of the age. (Matthew 28:18-20)

It couldn't be much clearer.

Whose kingdom are you building?

"God loves a hilarious giver." How hilarious are we?

You can't become a hilarious giver until you've settled two other issues. First, we are made in God's image for God's glory, and the only way we can reflect His glory is by making The Great Exchange, giving Him our lives so that He can give us His life—so that it is His life in us that is shining forth. And second, God is the treasure hidden in a field—we joyously go and surrender all that we have in order that we might know Him. We covered both of these points in the previous section.

Only now is it possible to begin seeing ourselves as God sees us. We are citizens of His heavenly kingdom (Philippians 3:20). We are Christ's ambassadors who are here to represent the interests of our King (2 Corinthians 5:20). We are not here to befriend the world, which would be treasonous

(James 4:4). On the contrary, we are to live our lives as aliens and strangers (1 Peter 2:11). We are just passing through, like pilgrims on a journey. Randy Alcorn, in his excellent book *Money, Possessions, and Eternity*, describes it this way.

> The pilgrim is unattached. He is a traveler—not a settler—acutely aware that the excessive accumulation of things can only distract him from what he is and does. Material things are valuable to the pilgrim, but only as they facilitate his mission. He knows they could become a god to grip him, and that if his eyes are on the visible they will be drawn away from the invisible.
>
> Does the pilgrim mentality lead to a sour or cynical view of this present world? Precisely the opposite! It is the materialist, not the Christian pilgrim, who is the cynic. The typical citizen of this world doesn't derive true satisfaction from it. Materialists can't fully appreciate the joys and wonders of creation. It is the believer who can see his Creator's handiwork everywhere, who can truly see the beauty of mountains and rivers and waterfalls. No one appreciates creation like he who knows the Creator. No one can appreciate a good meal like those who love the one who provided it. No one can enjoy marriage like the one who knows its Architect and Builder and who understands what intimacy is.
>
> One of the greatest joys the Christian pilgrim finds in this world is in those moments it reminds him of the next, his true home. He has not seen this place, but he has read about it, and he lives with the exhilarating assurance that his beloved is making it ready for him this very moment (John 14:2-3).

In the truest sense, Christian pilgrims have the best of both worlds. We have joy whenever this world reminds us of the next, and we take solace whenever it does not. We have the promise of a new heaven and new earth, where the worst elements of this world—sorrow, pain, death, and the tears they produce—will be gone forever (Revelation 21:4). Yet we also know that the best elements of this world, the love, joy, wonder, worship, and beauty we have experienced here, will not be gone, but intensified and perfected in the remade world. . . .

In the last book of the *Chronicles of Narnia*, when the unicorn reaches Aslan's country he exclaimed, "I have come home at last! This is my real country! I belong here. This is the land I have been looking for all my life, though I never knew it till now. The reason why we loved the old Narnia is that it sometimes looked a little like this." (R. Alcorn, *Money, Possessions and Eternity* [Wheaton: Tyndale House, 1989], pp. 196-198. Used by permission.)

Investing that glorifies God is motivated solely by a desire to see *His* kingdom grow. May I share with you some of the truths from Scripture that...

...I try to keep in mind as I plan my small role in the growth of God's kingdom and the accomplishment of His purposes. Consider these truths with me:

▶ **God is the absolute owner of everything in the universe. Period.**

"To the Lord your God belongs the heavens, even the highest heavens, the earth and everything in it." (Deuteronomy

10:14) ◆ "Who has a claim against me that I must pay? Everything under heaven belongs to me." (Job 41:11) ◆ "Yours, O Lord, is the kingdom; you are exalted as head over all. Wealth and honor come from you; you are the ruler of all things." (1 Chronicles 29:11-12)

▶ **God's ownership of all things includes me. God is never less than the sovereign/creator; I am never more than His steward/creature.**

"The earth is the Lord's, and everything in it, the world, and all who live in it; for he founded it upon the seas and established it upon the waters." (Psalm 24:1-2) ◆ "Do you not know that your body is a temple of the Holy Spirit, who is in you, whom you have received from God? You are not your own; you were bought at a price. Therefore honor God with your body." (1 Corinthians 6:19-20)

▶ **Since I have nothing that was not given to me, I have no basis for pride, only gratitude.**

"For who makes you different from anyone else? What do you have that you did not receive?" (1 Corinthians 4:7) ◆ "For we brought nothing into the world, and we can take nothing out of it. But if we have food and clothing, we will be content with that." (1 Timothy 6:7-8) ◆ "And my God will meet all your needs according to his glorious riches in Christ Jesus." (Philippians 4:19)

▶ **I have management responsibilities of the goods I hold, not ownership rights. It's a lifelong calling that requires me to continually live with one eye on eternity.**

"So if you have not been trustworthy in handling worldly wealth, who will trust you with true riches? And if you have not been trustworthy with someone else's property, who will give you property of your own?" (Luke 16:11-12) ♦ "If anyone would come after me, he must deny himself and take up his cross and follow me. For whoever wants to save his life will lose it, but whoever loses his life for me will find it. What good will it be for a man if he gains the whole world, yet forfeits his soul?" (Matthew 16:24-26)

▶ **My primary management responsibility is to be available to God for Him to think, act, speak, write, and give through me so that His will is accomplished and His name is glorified.**

"If you remain in me and my words remain in you, ask whatever you wish, and it will be given you. This is to my Father's glory, that you bear much fruit." (John 15:7-8) ♦ "So whether you eat or drink or whatever you do, do it all for the glory of God." (1 Corinthians 10:31)

▶ **God has provided me with guidelines for how best to manage His wealth for His glory. For the most part, they are general rather than specific, which means I need to seek His wisdom continually in order to make wise choices.**

"If any of you lacks wisdom, he should ask God, who gives generously to all without finding fault, and it will be given to him. But when he asks, he must believe and not doubt, because he who doubts is like a wave of the sea, blown and tossed by the wind." (James 1:5-6) ♦ "For God did not give us a spirit of timidity, but a spirit of

power, and love, and of self-discipline." (2 Timothy 1:7)
◆ "All Scripture is God-breathed and is useful for teaching, rebuking, correcting and training in righteousness, so that the man of God may be thoroughly equipped for every good work." (2 Timothy 3:16-17)

▶ **My giving, insofar as possible, is done primarily in the sight of God rather than in view of men. It belongs to the "secret life" of the believer so that God will receive the glory.**

"Be careful not to do your 'acts of righteousness' before men, to be seen by them. If you do, you will have no reward from your Father in heaven. . . . But when you give to the needy, do not let your left hand know what your right hand is doing, so that your giving may be in secret. Then your Father, who sees what is done in secret, will reward you." (Matthew 6:1, 3)

▶ **Wealth is exceedingly dangerous and has a history of spiritually devastating those who seek it. It must be handled with great care.**

"People who want to get rich fall into temptation and a trap and into many foolish and harmful desires that plunge men into ruin and destruction. For the love of money is a root of all kinds of evil. Some people, eager for money, have wandered from the faith and pierced themselves with many griefs." (1 Timothy 6:9)
◆ "Command those who are rich in this present world not to be arrogant nor to put their hope in wealth, which is so uncertain, but to put their hope in God, who richly provides us with everything for our enjoyment." (1 Timothy 6:17)

▶ I'm called to live fully in each day, not in the future. Therefore, God evaluates the faithfulness of my management based on what I do with what I have now, not what I might do someday if I had more.

> "But seek first his kingdom and his righteousness, and all these things will be given to you as well. Therefore, do not worry about tomorrow." (Matthew 6:33-34) ♦ "His master replied, 'Well done, good and faithful servant! You have been faithful with a few things; I will put you in charge of many things. Come and share your master's happiness.' " (Matthew 25:21)

▶ I should manage with a sense of urgency. This inclines me toward giving what I can now rather than saving up in order to give more later. Later may be too late. This has implications for how much of my wealth I leave my children or put aside in charitable foundations.

> "Do you not say, 'Four months more and then the harvest'? I tell you, open your eyes and look at the fields! They are ripe for harvest. Even now the reaper draws his wages, even now he harvests the crop for eternal life." (John 4:35-36) ♦ "As long as it is day, we must do the work of him who sent me. Night is coming, when no one can work." (John 9:4) ♦ "The Lord is not slow in keeping his promise, as some understand slowness. He is patient with you, not wanting anyone to perish, but everyone to come to repentance. But the day of the Lord will come like a thief. . ." (2 Peter 3:9-10)

▶ God has built the law of sowing and reaping into the fabric of the universe. He can be trusted to pay me the

perfectly appropriate wage for my work.

"Remember this: Whoever sows sparingly will also reap sparingly, and whoever sows generously will also reap generously." (2 Corinthians 9:6) ◆ "We speak of God's secret wisdom, a wisdom that has been hidden and that God destined for our glory before time began. None of the rulers of this age understood it, for if they had, they would not have crucified the Lord of glory. However, as it is written: 'No eye has seen, no ear has heard, no mind has conceived what God has prepared for those who love him.' " (1 Corinthians 2:7-9)

▶ **Giving is an affair of the heart. God looks at our earnest intentions, not our gifts.**

"The Lord does not look at the things man looks at. Man looks at the outward appearance, but the Lord looks at the heart." (1 Samuel 16:7) ◆ "Each man should give what he has decided in his heart to give, not reluctantly or under compulsion, for God loves a cheerful [hilarious] giver. And God is able to make all grace abound to you, so that in all things at all times, having all that you need, you will abound in every good work." (2 Corinthians 9:7-8)

▶ **It is not difficult to lay aside earthly wealth when you have God as your treasure.**

"Do not be afraid, little flock, for your Father has been pleased to give you the kingdom. Sell your possessions and give to the poor. Provide purses for yourselves that will not wear out, a treasure in heaven that will not be exhausted, where no thief comes near and no moth destroys. For where your treasure is, there your heart will be also." (Luke 12:32-34)

God owns it all. He doesn't need our help or our money. The fact is we have nothing He needs...

...and He has everything that we need. Bob Benson, one of my favorite writers, had a way of telling humorous stories in simple ways that revealed great truths. In this one, he once again put things into perspective for us. (R. Benson, *See You at the House* [Nashville: Generoux, 1986], pp. 68-69. Used by permission.)

> Do you remember when they had old-fashioned Sunday School picnics? I do. As I recall, it was back in the "olden days," as my kids would say, back before they had air conditioning.
>
> They said, "We'll all meet at Sycamore Lodge in Shelby Park at 4:30 on Saturday. You bring your supper and we'll furnish the iced tea."
>
> But if you were like me, you came home at the last minute. When you got ready to pack your picnic, all you could find in the refrigerator was one dried up piece of baloney and just enough mustard in the bottom of the jar so that you got it all over your knuckles trying to get to it. And just two slices of stale bread to go with it. So you made your baloney sandwich and wrapped it in an old brown bag and went to the picnic.
>
> When it came time to eat, you sat at the end of a table and spread out your sandwich. But the folks who sat next to you brought a feast. The lady was a good cook and she had worked hard all day to get ready for the picnic. And she had fried chicken and baked beans and potato salad

and homemade rolls and sliced tomatoes and pickles and olives and celery. And two big homemade chocolate pies to top it off. That's what they spread out there next to you while you sat with your baloney sandwich.

But they said to you, "Why don't we just put it all together?"

"No, I couldn't do that. I couldn't even think of it," you murmured in embarrassment, with one eye on the chicken.

"Oh, come on, there's plenty of chicken and plenty of pie and plenty of everything. And we just love baloney sandwiches. Let's just put it all together."

And so you did and there you sat, eating like a king when you came like a pauper.

One day, it dawned on me that God had been saying just that sort of thing to me. "Why don't you take what you have and what you are, and I will take what I have and what I am, and we'll share it together." I began to see that when I put what I had and was and am and hope to be with what he is, I had stumbled upon the bargain of a lifetime.

I get to thinking sometimes, thinking of me sharing with God. When I think of how little I bring, and how much he brings and invites me to share, I know that I should be shouting to the housetops, but I am so filled with awe and wonder that I can hardly speak. I know that I don't have enough love or faith or grace or mercy or wisdom, but he does. He has all of those things in abundance and he says, "Let's just put it all together."

Consecration, denial, sacrifice, commitment, crosses were all kind of hard words to me, until I saw them in the light of sharing. It isn't just a case of me kicking in what I have because God is the biggest kid in the neighborhood and he wants it all for himself. He is saying, "Everything that I possess is available to you. Everything that I am and can be to a person, I will be to you."

When I think about it like that, it really amuses me to see somebody running along through life hanging on to their dumb bag with that stale baloney sandwich in it saying, "God's not going to get my sandwich! No, sirree, this is mine!" Did you ever see anybody like that—so needy—just about half-starved to death yet hanging on for dear life. It's not that God needs your sandwich. The fact is, you need his chicken.

Well, go ahead—eat your baloney sandwich, as long as you can. But when you can't stand its tastelessness or drabness any longer; when you get so tired of running your own life by yourself and doing it your way and figuring out all the answers with no one to help; when trying to accumulate, hold, grasp, and keep everything together in your own strength gets to be too big a load; when you begin to realize that by yourself you're never going to be able to fulfill your dreams, I hope you'll remember that it doesn't have to be that way.

You have been invited to something better, you know. You have been invited to share in the very being of God. ◆

3

Investing That Glorifies God Upholds His Righteousness

What man is wise enough to understand this? Who has been instructed by the Lord and can explain it? Why has the land been ruined and laid waste like a desert that no one can cross? The Lord said, "It is because they have forsaken my law, which I set before them; they have not obeyed me or followed my law." . . . This is what the Lord says: "Let not the wise man boast of his wisdom or the strong man boast of his strength or the rich man boast of his riches, but let him who boasts boast about this: that he understands and knows me, that I am the Lord, who exercises kindness, justice and righteousness on earth, for in these I delight," declares the Lord.
(Jeremiah 9:12-13, 23-24)

This matter of taking heed of the ethical implications of where we invest our money has been popularly called "socially responsible" investing.

I receive more questions asking for suggestions on where to find ethical investments than on any other single topic. I believe that the people writing have a genuine desire to please the Lord in every aspect of their lives, including their finances. They are seeking investments that adhere to the righteous standards of Scripture. They sincerely strive to be faithful stewards, and they believe they have a responsibility to be sure they do not lend economic support to those worldly forces in opposition to what they see as biblical values. I respect their heartfelt concerns.

Unfortunately, I must tell them I can be of no help. Why not? Because I know of no investments that are guaranteed to meet their criteria. *In my experience, there are no morally pure or completely righteous investments.* Let's look at some of the possibilities.

● **Bank savings accounts and certificates of deposit.**

It is possible that your bank has loaned money to help build such businesses as the local newspaper that aggressively attacks Christian home-schooling in its editorials, the chemical company that illegally dumps its waste in presently unpopulated areas, or the bookstore that has several racks of pornographic magazines right by the front door where even young children can see them. Or your bank may have loaned money to the abortion clinic that has become the largest in your state, the engineering company whose PAC contributions perpetuate corruption in local government, or the music store in the local mall that promotes music and videos that glamorize sexually destructive and drug-addicting life-styles. The possibilities are almost limitless; let your imagination run a little. Almost every business has bank loans to some degree. The question is not *if* your bank has made loans to businesses engaged in practices abhorrent to you, but rather *how many and for how much*. And where do the banks get the money to make these loans? From the savings put on deposit by trusting folks like you and me.

SOUTH SHORE BANK

If you'd like to see part of your savings go toward helping those in need, this bank has become nationally known for its efforts to finance inner city housing projects. It offers CDs at competitive rates, and carries FDIC protection. For more information on its savings rates and lending policies, call 312-288-1000.

● **U.S. government bonds, notes, and treasury bills.**

These are the investments that make it possible for our government to run the huge budget deficits that make inflation an ever-present fact of American life. Many who write on economics from a biblical perspective consider inflation to be a great evil because it constitutes theft by the government. Much has been written on that subject alone. In addition, however, start considering the many ways that govern-

ment spends our money. Whether promoting abortion, supporting artists who produce blasphemous or pornographic
exhibits, or undermining traditional family values through
humanistic education and welfare programs, there is much
for Christians to be concerned about. The one exception
would be the bond mutual funds that invest only in govern-
ment-backed GNMA mortgages (which provide capital for
people to purchase homes). Other than these, are government securities ethical investments?

● **Common stocks.**

How many of the Fortune 500 companies do you believe
are operated according to Christian principles from top to
bottom? That would mean the application of a biblical moral
ethic in *all* of the following: their hiring and firing decisions,
employee pay schedules, environmental impact policies, the
way they price their products or services, their borrowing
and lending decisions, and the whole of their advertising
and marketing strategies. I doubt you can find even one.

My point is that investors have limited choices. Whether you invest in a bank certificate of deposit, U.S. treasuries, or selected common stocks...

...you have virtually no control over the specific uses to
which your money is put *once you turn it loose*. We are "in the
world" and must function in it. Paul writes in 1 Corinthians
5:9-10, "I have written you in my letter not to associate with

sexually immoral people—not at all meaning the people of this world who are immoral, or the greedy and swindlers, or idolaters. In that case you would have to leave this world." Paul recognizes the impossibility of completely avoiding contact with the corrupt world we inhabit. My conclusion: You can't altogether avoid *incidental financial contact* with disagreeable causes in the course of your investing, but you can avoid lending them *meaningful support*.

Socially responsible investing (SRI) continues to grow as a force in the investment world.

According to a report in *Kiplinger's Personal Finance*, "less than a decade ago, $40 billion resided in socially screened

Fund Name	Abortion Concerns	Alcoholic Beverages	Animal Welfare	Casino Gambling	Defense Weapons
Amana Income		x		x	
Calvert Ariel Appreciation		x			x
Calvert Ariel Growth		x			x
Calvert Social Equity		x	x	x	x
Domini Social Equity		x		x	x
Dreyfus Third Century					
New Alternatives			x		x
Parnassus		x		x	x
Pax World		x		x	x
Progressive Environmental					x
Rightime Social Awareness					x
Timothy Plan	x	x		x	

SCREENING CRITERIA OF

portfolios; today the amount exceeds $700 billion, when you include institutional as well as individual investments. In just three years, the number of mutual funds that profess to be 'socially responsible' has doubled."

SRI mutual funds use a set of portfolio guidelines called "screens" to reflect their values. Most rely on avoidance screens which are designed to eliminate companies engaged in objectionable activities or practices. (This is probably the most common SRI approach, and is what most individual investors mean when they say they are interested in "ethical" investing.) As you might expect when it comes to drawing ethical boundaries, developing these screens involves many personal judgments on the part of the fund sponsor

LEADING SRI FUNDS

Environment Concerns	Labor Practices	Nuclear Energy	Pornography Concerns	South Africa	Tobacco Products	Phone
			x		x	800-728-8762
x		x		x	x	800-368-2748
x		x		x	x	800-368-2748
x	x	x		x	x	800-368-2748
x		x		x	x	800-762-6814
x				x	x	800-782-6620
x	x	x		x		516-466-0808
x		x		x	x	800-999-3505
x		x		x	x	800-767-1729
x	x	x		x		800-275-2382
x		x		x		800-242-1421
			x		x	800-TIM-PLAN

and portfolio manager. To help you see where the leading SRI stock funds have chosen to take their stands, I prepared the table on pages 38-39. The chart also shows that the new Timothy Plan fund filled a void in the lineup of ethical funds when it became the first to specifically use abortion-related activities as an avoidance screen.

Even without social screening, I believe that mutual funds are acceptable investing vehicles for the same reason that bank savings accounts and T-bills are acceptable: The role your investment plays is absolutely insignificant in relation to the size of the problem areas. In fact, it is too small to even be called "support" at all in the usual sense, as I will soon demonstrate.

It's interesting to me that many investors have a difficult time with the ethics of investing in stock mutual funds, yet don't give a second thought...

...to the morality of building sizable bank savings account and treasury bill holdings. Consistency would call for demanding ethical purity in those investments as well.

Let's look at your bank, for example. Assume that it has $100 million in loans outstanding, and that you would perhaps find $2 million of them seriously objectionable (if you knew about them). Further assume that you have a $5,000 CD on deposit there. Your CD represents 1/200 of 1% of the bank's total loans outstanding. That means that for every $10,000 your bank loans out, you "contribute" 50 cents to the loan. Is your CD an ethical investment? If you are looking for absolute purity, then it doesn't qualify because 2% of the loan portfolio fails your ethics test. But is your meager role statistically meaningful? Obviously not. That's why I would consider the CD investment acceptable.

I won't spend time reviewing the extent to which investing in U.S. securities (T-bills, notes, bonds, and government-only money market funds) support the federal government's spending programs. The relatively minuscule size of an individual's holdings in relation to the absolutely massive size of the federal budget is obvious to everyone.

Now, let's apply the same logic to the purchase of mutual funds. Consider this. A mutual fund rarely owns even one-tenth of 1% of a given company's stock. Furthermore, few investors would ever hold as much as one-tenth of 1% of any one mutual fund's assets. Therefore, owning a mutual fund limits the average investor to holding *less than one one-millionth of any one company's shares*. The ownership effect is nil.

Here's an example of how this works. One of the Vanguard funds recommended in my newsletter held 366,000 shares of stock in Philip Morris, the huge tobacco company with more than 925 million shares outstanding. This means that the fund owns about 1/2,500 of Philip Morris. Let's assume you invest $5,000 in this Vanguard fund; how much ownership in Philip Morris would this give you? You would own 1/70,000 of a fund which owns 1/2,500 of Philip Morris.

Congratulations! That makes you the owner of 1/175,000,000 (that's one part in 175 million!) of Philip Morris. Such investment hardly qualifies as support.

We want our drinking water to be clean, but we don't demand that it be sterile. We all would like clean air, but we don't walk around wearing oxygen masks. If we accept 99.9% purity when it comes to matters of life and health, doesn't it seem reasonable to apply the same standards to material pursuits like investing? At this point, you may be concluding that I am unconcerned about corporate ethics and using one's economic influence to battle immoral forces. If so, you misunderstand my point. It's not that I want you to be less radical in this area. I want you to become *more* radical.

I want to encourage you to expand your thinking beyond boycotting the purchase of a company's stock toward *boycotting the purchase of their goods and services.*

In November 1990, *The Wall Street Journal* ran an article captioned "Facing a Boycott, Many Companies Bend." It reported that boycotts "have become increasingly common as more and more groups (representing consumers, environmentalists, religions and others) have targeted individual companies" requesting them to change their policies. Boycotters are finding increasingly receptive listeners at major corporations for two reasons. First, it only takes a modest decline in sales (5-10%) to adversely affect their profits. And second, boycotters often come from two-income families in the high-spending "nest building" stage of life—a highly desirable demographic group of customers.

In short, boycotts work! One of the most influential consumer organizations is Christian Leaders for Responsible Television, a coalition of approximately 1,600 denominational and parachurch groups. Finding the major television networks completely indifferent to the concerns of Americans who hold traditional biblical values of morality, this coalition turned their attention to the corporate sponsors who make the programming possible.

This coalition was an outgrowth of the pioneering work done by Rev. Don Wildmon, founder of the American Family Association. The AFA is right to be concerned about the moral decline of our society and its contribution to the destruction of the family. Falsely accused by some of "censorship," they have a boycotting philosophy that I find right on target: The networks are free to show whatever programming *they* wish, companies are free to sponsor whatever programming *they* wish, and consumers are free to support and patronize whomever *we* wish.

Far be it from us as Christians, who are responsible for handling God's wealth for God's glory, that we should provide essential financial support to the very people and institutions whose activities are undermining the biblical values we hold dear. Consider how the moral foundations of our society have been shaken in recent decades—can you doubt that we are under attack? We are in a war over whose values will prevail in America, not only for the rest of this century but for the next. Not just for our children, but for their children. Yet some of us routinely and indifferently subsidize those who most despise us.

We have an obligation to withhold support, insofar as possible, from those businesses whose corporate activities either actively mock or passively undermine the biblical values that God has given as the basis for righteousness in society. This can be done most effectively by boycotting their products and services; withholding investment support from their stocks and bonds can also be helpful if done in a concerted fashion. Both of these strategies should play a central role in the spending and investing decisions of every follower of Christ.

Investing that glorifies God upholds His righteousness.

In this booklet, we have discussed why investing that glorifies God acknowledges His sovereignty (God owns it all), values His majesty (*He* is the treasure), and builds His kingdom (we are to manage His wealth for His glory). If you are committed to making money-management decisions that reflect your firm convictions about those first three truths, you will have no problem understanding and believing this one.

> This then, is how you should pray: "Our Father in heaven, hallowed be your name, *your kingdom come,* your will be done on earth as it is in heaven." (Matthew 6:9-10)

It naturally follows that you will feel a solemn obligation to use your financial leverage to the maximum in order that His righteousness is revealed and upheld. No one will need to persuade you that it is a good thing. You will be grieved to think it would be otherwise.

> Righteous are you, O Lord, and your laws are right. The statutes you have laid down are righteous; they are fully trustworthy. *My zeal wears me out, for my enemies ignore your words.* Your promises have been thoroughly tested, and your servant loves them. (Psalm 119:137-140)

Our God is righteous. Because He is righteous, we must regard what belongs to Him, such as the money we manage, as consecrated for righteous purposes. The thought of turning God's wealth over to His enemies, to use against His glorious name and His church, should be abhorrent to the faithful steward. We must take care to avoid financing activities that lead others into temptation and sin.

> Whoever welcomes a little child like this in my name welcomes me. But if anyone causes one of these little ones who believe in me to sin, it would be better for him to have a large millstone hung around his neck and to be drowned in the depths of the sea. *Woe to the world because of the things that cause people to sin! Such things must come, but woe to the man through whom they come!* (Matthew 18:5-7) ◆

Investing That Glorifies God Seeks His Wisdom

4

The law of the Lord is perfect, reviving the soul.
The statutes of the Lord are trustworthy, making
wise the simple. The precepts of the Lord are right,
giving joy to the heart. The commands of the Lord
are radiant, giving light to the eyes. The fear of the
Lord is pure, enduring forever. The ordinances of
the Lord are sure and altogether righteous.
They are more precious than gold, than much
pure gold; they are sweeter than honey, than
honey from the comb. By them is your servant
warned; in keeping them there is great reward. . . .
May the words of my mouth and the meditation of
my heart be pleasing in your sight, O Lord, my
Rock and my Redeemer. (Psalm 19:7-14)

The commencement speaker at the University of California School of Business had these words of advice: *"Greed is all right. Greed is healthy...*

...*You can be greedy and still feel good about yourself. Greed works."* The comments reportedly were received with laughter and applause by the new graduates. The speaker was Ivan Boesky, a millionaire hundreds of times over. Not too many months later, he was sent to prison for violating securities laws in his relentless quest to acquire even more.

How much is enough, anyway? Obviously, for some, there's no such thing as ever having "enough." It's not because they have material wants that are left unmet; Ivan Boesky couldn't possibly have spent, no matter how extravagant his personal life-style, all the money he had. There are those for whom money represents success, status, superiority, and power. They are pursuing it in a doomed attempt to fill an inner emptiness. But that emptiness is like a black hole; no matter how much you put in, it never fills with light. Ironically, Boesky's very life gave the lie to his words. Greed, it turns out, doesn't work after all.

Fortunately, we Christians already understand this. Greed may be something to watch out for...

...when doing business with "the world," but followers of Christ are not like that. We can relax with them. *They* would never take advantage of us, right?... Right?... Hello?...

Perhaps I imagine that my question is being received with less than thunderous agreement because I routinely receive letters from readers of my newsletter that contain horror stories of the various financial atrocities committed against them by people they trusted to have their best interests at heart. They met these people at church, a couples' Bible study, through a Christian friend, or through some other association that would lead them to believe the person was trustworthy. Unfortunately, limiting your business transactions solely to Christians is no assurance that everything will work out happily ever after.

That reminds me, have I ever told you about my $100,000 tennis racket?

During my tenure with Campus Crusade, the idea struck me how great it would be if I found competent Christian people to invest with. They would perform the day-to-day work of the investment projects, and eventually we could live off the income and be free to continue devoting our time to ministry pursuits.

Well, it wasn't long (wouldn't you know it?) before I was approached about investing in a real-estate project. I was introduced by a co-worker to a friend of his who was a developer (let's call him Dugan) in the greater San Diego area. He and his partner Roberts needed temporary financing on one of their projects until their permanent construction loan was approved. They were willing to pay a healthy rate of interest, personally guarantee the loan, plus pledge some stock Dugan owned as additional collateral. They had done other projects previously and had development experience. I verified with the lending institution that their loan request had, indeed, received approval, pending receipt of their pro forma financial statements.

Dugan and his wife were super people; you couldn't help but like them. They entertained us at their country club. They invited us over for friendly tennis (Dugan gave me one of his rackets so I could practice regularly). Since we were living away from Kentucky, they even included us in their plans for Thanksgiving dinner. We were practically family! So everything seemed to line up pretty well. And what seemed to confirm it was that the opportunity to invest with a Christian had come along just when it seemed the natural direction to go.

You know something went wrong, or I wouldn't own a tennis racket that cost me $100,000. Here's the sorry sequence of events.

❶ Through negligence, Dugan missed the deadline for submitting the financial statements to the lender, and they lost their construction loan.

❷ The economy was going through a downturn, and they could not get another loan commitment. The project never got off the ground. Fortunately, I still had the personal guarantees of the Dugans and the Robertses.

❸ Roberts died suddenly of a heart attack. Being a sensitive kind of guy who doesn't want to invade a widow's grief,

I let some time go by before asking for her share of my money. While I was being noble, her late husband's attorney was helping her "hide" her assets; she eventually produced a financial statement that made her appear penniless. Curiously, six months after the sudden departure of Mr. Roberts, the former Mrs. Roberts married the attorney.

❹ Mr. Dugan and his wife filed for protection under the bankruptcy laws and moved to northern California. I never heard from them again.

❺ The stock Dugan pledged was in a land development company that was operated and controlled by his brother (who was reportedly furious that the stock had been pledged and was now outside the family). The brother later told me that things were going so well that my stock holdings would be worth $1 million within three years. This was a little optimistic; the company expanded too quickly, eventually lost its land holdings, and disappeared into bankruptcy never-never land.

What did I learn from this misadventure? I learned not to make certain unwarranted assumptions...

...when dealing with fellow Christians. First, I assumed that because Dugan had experience and seemed to know what he was doing, he was competent. I didn't really check him out. It turned out that his personable style made him competent only as a promoter. It was of little help in the nitty-gritty of day-to-day details. Second, I assumed that these were people of integrity. They seemed so *sincere!* Yet they readily hid behind the bankruptcy laws to avoid repaying the money they had so earnestly besought me to loan them. Boy, had I learned an important lesson! I wouldn't make *those* mistakes again. I would make *new* ones.

This brings me to the story of my $50,000 Swiss army knife key ring.

Jack, a good Christian friend, brought it back as a souvenir from one of the frequent business trips to Europe he made for a business deal we were in together. I won't go into all the details here. I'll just skip to the new lessons I learned about *other* unwarranted assumptions you shouldn't make. First, I assumed that all the facts of the deal were exactly as Jack had represented them to me. (By the way, note that I no longer needed go-betweens to introduce me to people like Dugan — by this time I was going directly to my close personal friends to lose my money.) I know that Jack truly believed—evidently too optimistically—everything he was telling me. The point is that I would never have accepted the story just on the word of a stranger. I would have expected documented proof of all the facts. With Jack, my guard was completely down.

Second, I assumed that because I could trust my friend, the usual precautions didn't apply. In another booklet in this series (*Investments That Fit You: How to Develop a Strategy Based on Your Personality Type*), I gave five guidelines for making investment decisions. In this one deal, I broke the first four of the guidelines without hesitation.

Guideline 1: The right portfolio move is one that is consistent with a specific, biblically sound long-term strategy you've adopted. The deal wasn't consistent with my long-term strategy because I didn't have one.

Guideline 2: The right portfolio move is one where you've taken plenty of time to pray as you consider trusted, experienced Christian counsel. I didn't take much time to pray about it or seek counsel from others.

Guideline 3: The right portfolio move is one you understand. I never really understood the logistics of the deal or why it was supposed to work the way it was.

Guideline 4: The right portfolio move is one that is prudent under the circumstances. Does it pass the "common sense" test? The investment totally failed the common sense test of prudence.

In retrospect, it's so improbable that it could have worked that I'm embarrassed to even tell you what it was about. In short, my trust was totally in the knowledge and experience of my friend. The reason I didn't give the guidelines a thought is because I hadn't learned to apply biblical principles to financial decision making at that point. (Larry Burkett was just getting his ministry started in those days. Larry, where were you when I needed you?) This happened in 1976, and I was still flying on gut instinct.

I hope you appreciate the "school" I went to in learning these lessons which I'm passing on to you for the unbelievably low price of this booklet. The tuition for this one cost me $50,000 (or just $49,990 if you want to count the $10 value of my Swiss army knife key ring).

Before you can consistently apply God's wisdom, you must erase from your mind the preconceived ideas you have about what it means to be a "savvy" investor. If you're like most people...

...you have accumulated years of impressions concerning financial wizardry from the secular world. You may be under the assumption that it's a sign of financial sophistication to borrow to invest, frequently adjust your portfolio in response to changing world events, always seek the maximum return, or invest for short-term results.

Such tactics may occasionally be profitable, but more often they are self-destructive. In any event, they go against God's wisdom as given us in His word. We need to learn to think with new minds in order to understand His will.

> I urge you, brothers, in view of God's mercy, to offer your bodies as living sacrifices, holy and pleasing to God — this is your spiritual act of worship. Do not conform any longer to the pattern of this world, but be transformed *by the renewing of your mind.* Then you will be able to test and approve what God's will is — his good, pleasing and perfect will. (Romans 12:1-2)

PRYOR'S RULES FOR EVALUATING INVESTMENTS THAT SEEK YOU OUT

Rule #1
Assume the investment is being offered to you by a representative of Ivan Boesky. It's not that the person soliciting your investment is likely to be as greedy or dishonest as Boesky. I just want to help you to stay alert and not repeat the mistake of making unwarranted assumptions. All the remaining rules logically follow from this one.

Rule #2
Ask the individual to put everything of importance (like representations of risk, how much money you're guaranteed to make, how long it's all going to take) in written form. Assume nothing.

Rule #3
Check his facts thoroughly. Ask someone you trust, who has nothing to do with the deal, to help you. Assume nothing.

Rule #4
Verify his track record. Contact other investors with whom he's done business. Assume nothing.

Rule #5
Ask for personal character references, including one from his pastor. Then call the people and talk with them personally. Assume nothing.

Rule #6
If you decide to go ahead, put the entire deal in writing, signed by all concerned, so that you have a legally enforceable position. Handshake deals are out.

Rule #7
Make absolutely, positively no exceptions to Rules #1 through #6. And, oh yes, assume nothing.

As we renew our minds, we not only see more clearly who God is; we also gain insight into our own natures.

My observation that investors are their own worse enemies stems not only from my 17 years of practical experience but also is confirmed by God's Word. Given our fallen natures, it would be surprising if we *weren't* the primary problem we face when investing. Consider for a moment the kind of people we are. The failings of our wisdom, our motives, our emotions, and our clarity of vision are well documented in the Scriptures.

▶ **Our wisdom is flawed.**

Let no person deceive himself. If any one among you supposes that he is wise in this age—let him discard his worldly discernment and recognize himself as dull, stupid, and foolish, without true learning and scholarship; let him become a fool that he may become really wise. For this world's wisdom is foolishness — absurdity and stupidity — with God. (1 Corinthians 3:18-19; AMPLIFIED)

▶ **Our motivations are impure.**

The heart is deceitful above all things, and it is exceedingly perverse and corrupt and severely, mortally sick! Who can know, perceive, understand, be acquainted with his own heart and mind? (Jeremiah 17:9; AMPLIFIED)

▶ **Our emotions are powerful.**

For I know that nothing good dwells within me, that is, in my flesh. I can will what is right, but I cannot perform it—I have the intention and urge to do what is right, but no power to carry it out. . . (Romans 7:18; AMPLIFIED)

▶ Our vision is limited.

Come now, you who say, Today or tomorrow we will go into such and such a city and spend a year there to carry on our business and make money. Yet you do not know the least thing about what may happen tomorrow. . . . You boast falsely in your presumption and your self-conceit. (James 4:13-14, 16; AMPLIFIED)

As we renew our minds, we can begin to put proper boundaries in place that not only define our Christian priorities and values but *will also serve to protect us from the markets and ourselves. The reason for having an individualized investment strategy is to provide these needed boundaries.*

You begin by acknowledging that you need help. Your financial life has no central focus. You make decisions as situations arise based on what you've read is best, what a friend says is best, or just by throwing a dart and hoping for the best. You find yourself pulled in all directions, looking something like this:

 Flawed Wisdom 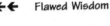 Impure Motives   Powerful Emotions   Limited Vision

A strategy helps *contain and focus* your impulses by providing boundaries. It boxes you in and takes away your freedom to do what you might want. But it offers a new kind of freedom—the freedom to do what you should. It gives you a sense of perspective and a new way of knowing what's "right" for you. The graphic illustration on the next page shows the four boundaries to a focused investment strategy: objective, mechanical criteria for decision-making, a portfolio that is broadly diversified, a long-term, get-rich-slow perspective, and a manager's (rather than owner's) mentality. Let's now look at how these boundaries come into play in practical ways in everyday life situations.

Boundary One: Using mechanical guidelines rather than your own intuition and judgment.

> He who trusts in himself is a fool, but he who walks in wisdom is kept safe. (Proverbs 28:26) ♦ But the fruit of the Spirit is... self-control. (Galatians 5:22-23)

Mechanical guidelines require that you develop objective criteria you follow for your buying and selling decisions. One example would be adopting one of the four investing temperaments suggested in my booklet, *Investments That Fit You*. The allocations that are laid out for you provide explicit, objective boundaries to help you diversify according to your risk tolerance and age. They help make your investment shopping purposeful. Such boundaries protect you from giving in to sales presentations on some "really attractive" investment that you don't need at present.

Another example would be setting value criteria for timing your stock buying and selling. You might decide to take profits in any stock once its price/earnings ratio reaches a certain predetermined level. Or you might look for underpriced stocks using the price/dividend or price/book ratios.

Knowing when to sell is much more difficult than knowing when to buy. The momentum approach for evaluating mutual fund performance explained in my book *Sound Mind Investing* is another way of using mechanical guidelines. It gives you objective reasons for selecting funds, and is especially useful for knowing when it may be time to replace a fund.

Mechanical rules can help you control your losses. When you buy a stock or fund that doesn't perform as you hope, it can be difficult emotionally to admit it didn't work out. People often hold onto weak com-

MANAGER MENTALITY

MECHANICAL GUIDELINES

LONG-TERM GET RICH SLOW

BROAD DIVERSIFICATION

Impure Motives

Flawed Wisdom

Limited Vision

Powerful Emotions

panies for years hoping to sell when they can "get even." This is a form of denial; the loss has already taken place. This emotional trap can be avoided by a mechanical guideline that says, "I'll sell if it drops x% from where I bought it because if it gets that low, there's a probability I misjudged the situation."

Dollar-cost-averaging is a strategy that uses mechanical guidelines to help you know how much to invest and when. The discipline imposed by such a program is helpful because our judgment tends to be unduly influenced by news events of the moment. There will always be bad news, but news is rarely as bad or good as it might first appear. These guidelines protect you from overreacting (along with everyone else) to the crisis or euphoria of the moment.

The markets go to extremes because they are driven by emotions, not reason. Also, professional money managers are afraid of getting left behind and looking bad (they want job security too, you know), so they go along with the crowd and panic like everyone else. Mechanical guidelines help harness the powerful emotions that often cause investors to do precisely the wrong thing at precisely the wrong time. Mechanical rules may appear dull, but that's actually a virtue— the most successful market strategies tend to be dull because they are measured, not spontaneous.

Before leaving the subject of emotions, may I suggest another idea about how to remain objective? Don't give investment advice to friends and family, and don't tell them what your investment holdings are. It's not a question of secrecy; it's the tendency you'll have to lose your objectivity about the investments in question. It's important to remain flexible and follow your guidelines, right? But how can you take a loss in this great stock or fund that you've told everybody about? You might find yourself thinking, "This is humiliating. Everybody will think I'm an idiot. Better to at least wait until I can get out at 'break-even' so I can save face." Oops, that's exactly the kind of emotional decision-making you want to avoid.

Boundary Two: Building a broadly diversified portfolio to protect against the uncertainties of the future.

Give portions to seven, yes to eight, for you do not know what disaster may come upon the land. (Ecclesiastes 11:2)
♦ But the fruit of the Spirit is. . . peace. (Galatians 5:22)

Acknowledging our limited vision says, "I don't know what the future holds. The financial media don't know. My stockbroker doesn't know. Investment newsletter writers don't know. Nobody knows." Since we don't (and can't) know the future, we can never know in advance with certainty which investments will turn out most profitably. That is the rationale for diversifying—spreading out your portfolio into various areas so that you won't be overinvested in any hard-hit areas and you'll have at least some investments in the most rewarding areas. Once you accept that "nobody knows," here are some of the things you're free to do:

● Ask hard and skeptical questions of anyone trying to sell you an investment. Make the person support and document every assertion, promise, or guarantee. You don't need to let him intimidate you anymore, because you know the truth: Nobody knows for sure, no matter how confident he sounds, whether what he is recommending will truly turn out to be the best for you.

● Ignore all forecasts by the "experts." There's a kind of Newton's Law of Motion for economics: For every forecast by a group of experts with impressive credentials, there's an equal and opposite forecast by another group of experts with equally impressive credentials. Besides, if you've ever noticed, most forecasts seem to assume that the current trends (whatever they are) will continue. If they *were* to have any value, we'd need to know when the current trends will be reversed.

● Ignore the media's explanations for why the markets are acting as they are. Almost every item of economic news has both positive and negative implications, depending on what you want. For example, lower interest rates are good news if you're a borrower, bad news if you're a saver; a strong dollar is good news for importers, bad news for exporters. When the news is released, the media watches the markets' reactions. The next day, they merely emphasize *that aspect of the news* that the markets paid most attention to. If lower rates cause the stock market to go up, the media says it's because low rates are good for the economy; if the market goes down, the media says its because low rates encourage renewed inflation.

You should recognize that the media's explanations of market behavior are merely after-the-fact rationalizations.

● Ignore most of the direct mail that you receive promoting an investment advisory letter. I'm talking primarily about the ones with the bold-letter "hype" that promise easy or guaranteed profits due to their consistent accuracy in making predictions about the markets. Such claims are meaningless—every newsletter writer is correct in some of his expectations and wrong about others. Some are right more than they're wrong, but nobody is consistently right. There's always a possibility that you can lose your money in the markets—it's irresponsible to imply otherwise. Such claims by any newsletter writer (or broker or anyone else) should immediately raise a red flag in your mind and call his credibility into question.

Boundary Three: Developing a long-term, get-rich-slow perspective.

> Dishonest money dwindles away, but he who gathers money little by little makes it grow. (Proverbs 13:11) ◆
> But the fruit of the Spirit is. . . patience. (Galatians 5:22)

Fewer things cause investors more losses than a short-term, get-rich-quick orientation to decision-making. Patience, a fruit of the Spirit, is in short supply among investors today. Many have the attention span of a strobe light. A long-term view is extremely productive when investing; such a perspective has three major benefits:

❶ It allows you time to do first things first. I've already discussed the importance of being debt-free before proceeding into stocks, bonds, and other investments (other than those in your retirement plans). In the face of market setbacks, a long-term view says, "I'm investing with my surplus funds. This is no threat to my immediate well-being. I've got time to wait for the recovery."

❷ It allows you to let those "once-in-a-lifetime, you-don't-want-to-miss-this-one-but-you-must-act-now" deals go by. You've got plenty of time, and you don't want to invest in anything you haven't had time to carefully investigate and pray about. Trust me—there's always another day and another "great deal."

❸ It allows you to be more relaxed when your judgment turns out less than perfect (surprise!). For example, those times when the stock you just bought goes lower (which it always will) or the one you just sold goes even higher (which it always will). Why let that frustrate you? In your saner moments, you know it's extremely unlikely you're going to buy at the exact low or sell at the exact high. Taking the long view says, "It doesn't matter whether I bought at $14 when I could have bought at $12. The important thing is that I followed my plan. Over time, I know my plan will get me where I want to go."

Boundary Four: Accepting management responsibility for your decisions, which leads

you to acquire a knowledge of the basics and seek counsel when making important decisions.

> Every prudent man acts out of knowledge, but a fool exposes his folly. (Proverbs 13:16) ♦ But the fruit of the Spirit is. . . faithfulness. (Galatians 5:22)

Ultimately, you are accountable for what happens. You have been given a responsibility that you cannot delegate away. You can delegate authority to someone else to make certain investment decisions, but you cannot delegate your responsibility for the results that come from those decisions.

Once you "own" this fact, you will take your management obligations even more seriously. Many Christians do not see themselves as "investors" simply because they don't have large stock portfolios. I believe they have a misconception as to what investing involves. *Investing decisions involve deciding what you will do without today in order that you might have more of something later.*

Taking a second job (sacrifice time) or cutting back on your spending (sacrifice convenience/luxury) in order to get debt-free (gain peace of mind and freedom) is an investing decision. Buying a used car rather than a new one (sacrifice status and ego) in order to start saving for a house someday (gain shelter and security) is an investing decision. Keeping your savings in money market funds instead of bond funds (sacrifice yield) in order to have your principal safe (gain stability and flexibility) is an investing decision.

Knowing that managing this part of your life responsibly is a God-given task will help you to become more realistic about your needs in four areas:

▶ **More realistic about your need for additional knowledge.** You accept that you must learn certain financial and investing basics. You can't just say, "Oh, I don't have the time (or interest or intellect) for that." You understand that some study will be necessary.

▶ **More realistic about the limitations of what investing can accomplish for you.** As you study, you learn that rates of return over time tend to be in the 8%-12% range, not 15%-20% as many imagine. The idea that you will readily make large returns to bail you out of your problems is a dream. And mixed in that 8%-12% average will be good years (20% to 30%) and bad years (-10% to -20%). It's not a smooth road.

▶ **More realistic about the strengths and weaknesses of the investment industry.** It does not have your best interests, first and foremost, at heart. It is awash in conflicts of interest (brokers get paid for selling securities, publishers get paid for selling magazines, financial networks get paid for attracting viewers). Your naïveté will diminish as you develop a healthy skepticism. On the plus side, America is still a land of great economic opportunity for those who are willing to diligently apply themselves and who do not easily give up.

▶ **More realistic about the markets themselves.** You'll no longer believe that "the pros" know something you don't, and you'll see the widely erratic swings as being evidence of emotionalism rather than calm reason. You'll discover there are few absolutes, other than preservation of your capital and survival, to guide you as you navigate the tumultuous storms and cross-currents.

These doses of realism will be healthy for you.

Investing that glorifies God seeks His wisdom.

The wisdom found in God's Word is there for our protection and His glory. In financial matters, it points to God Himself as our true treasure and helps us see that *we* are the ones who suffer when we seek our treasure elsewhere.

Let's not settle for the creation when we can have the Creator.

Let's not settle for the temporal when we can have the eternal.

Let's not settle for knowing man's wisdom when we can know God's wisdom—Christ Himself.

> Where is the wise man? Where is the scholar? Where is the philosopher of this age? Has not God made foolish the wisdom of the world? For since in the wisdom of God the world through its wisdom did not know him, God was pleased through the foolishness of what was preached to save those who believe. Jews demand miraculous signs and Greeks look for wisdom, but we preach Christ crucified: a stumbling block to Jews and foolishness to Gentiles, but to

those whom God has called, both Jews and Greeks, *Christ the power of God and the wisdom of God*. For the foolishness of God is wiser than man's wisdom, and the weakness of God is stronger than man's strength. Brothers, think of what you were when you were called. Not many of you were wise by human standards; not many were influential; not many were of noble birth. But God chose the foolish things of the world to shame the wise; God chose the weak things of the world to shame the strong. He chose the lowly things of this world and the despised things—and the things that are not—to nullify the things that are, so that no one may boast before him. It is because of him that you are in *Christ Jesus, who has become for us wisdom from God*—that is, our righteousness, holiness and redemption. Therefore, as it is written: "Let him who boasts boast in the Lord." (1 Corinthians 1:20-31)

May God grant us the grace to know Him. To seek for nothing else, and to settle for nothing less. ♦

Investing That Glorifies God Enjoys His Blessings

Delight yourself also in the Lord, and He will give you the desires and secret petitions of your heart. Commit your way to the Lord—roll and repose [each care of] your load on Him; trust (lean on, rely on and be confident) in Him, and He will bring it to pass.
(Psalm 37:4-5 AMPLIFIED)

The Scripture says, No man who believes in Him—who adheres to, relies on and trusts in Him—will [ever] be put to shame or be disappointed. For there is no distinction between Jew and Greek. The same Lord is Lord over all [of us], and He generously bestows His riches upon all who call upon Him in faith.
(Romans 10:11-12 AMPLIFIED)

"Dad, today I bought all these baseball cards at the flea market for $15, and my price guide says they're worth $25! I've already made $10!"

Have you ever tried explaining to your children that a thing is worth only what someone is willing to pay for it? And that unless they intend to become dealers in baseball cards, it's highly unlikely they will ever be able to get their $15 back, let alone come out $10 ahead? My boys always brushed off such explanations as being naive and hopelessly out of touch with the financial realities which govern baseball cards (or stamps, comic books, etc). The fact that I had a college degree in economics and was a full-fledged investment adviser carried no weight whatsoever. They regarded me with a kind of bemused tolerance. ("Poor dad, he means well.")

Children aren't the only ones who sometimes have a difficult time with the concept of value. I do, too. I have concluded that I have very little ability to discern what is valuable in life and what isn't. I don't always see clearly which experiences are blessings and which ones do me harm. In fact, it's probably safe to say that I really don't even know — with complete certainty — what I truly want.

That's why one of the most exciting steps I can take is to pray and ask God for things. I neither know which requests He'll grant nor have the slightest insight into how He'll work through circumstances in granting those requests He does. But I'm learning it's usually in the most improbable and unexpected ways.

By the mid-1980s, my business partner and I had built our advisory business to what could fairly be called a "successful" level. Our investment performance results...

...had frequently placed in the top 5% among advisers nationwide. Money goes where it's treated best, and we had attracted enough clients that we were both taking home six-figure incomes. Plus, I still had time for my ministry interests. All in all, things were working out pretty well.

Then I entered a period where I seemed to have the reverse Midas touch. In about a three-year span, my financial roof fell in thanks to a variety of unrelated events: a home that took three years to sell, unprecedented losses in my personal futures trading account, and a costly business venture in South Carolina, to name a few.

The summer of 1987 was the worst period of my business life. In April, with the Dow around 2,300, we had sold all stock funds and placed our clients 100% into money market funds. We did this because we felt the market had risen too far, too fast. The environment had become one of high risk. As the Dow continued to make new highs over the summer months (and everybody "knew" it was going to 3,000), we began losing clients to other firms who had no such reservations about risk. Our warnings to our departing clients fell on deaf ears. I'm sure many felt we were out of touch with the realities of the market. In truth, they and their new money managers were the ones out of touch, as the October crash violently demonstrated. In a single day, the Dow Jones dropped more than 500 points, and it did not recover to its former level for two years. The crash vindicated our caution, but it was too late to stabilize our client base. The defections dealt a major blow to our company and required Doug and me to take drastic salary cuts and make other expense-related adjustments.

So there I was facing substantial business and personal financial pressures that I would never have dreamed of a few years earlier. And I was asking...

..."Lord, why is this happening to me? I travel and speak in Your name. I work and give diligently for Your causes. How come You're treating me like this? Please get me out of this mess. Please reassure me that everything's going to be all right. But most of all, please let me know that You're still here with me."

You know what the Lord said to me? Nothing. I've never heard from the Lord *directly* in all my life. I know some people who have, but I never have. However, the Lord does speak to me by giving me ideas and impressions as I read and meditate in His Word. And over time the answer to my pleading question came. It was as if He said:

"You prayed that you could become mature, didn't you? I'm teaching you how to depend on Me more."

"You prayed for more faith, didn't you? I'm giving you a chance to trust Me more."

"You prayed that you could be used to minister to others, didn't you? I'm training you so you can serve Me more."

"You prayed that you might know Me better, didn't you? I'm helping you to seek Me more."

"You prayed that you might glorify Me with your life, didn't you? I'm refining you more."

When we pray prayers that contain such "spiritual" requests, we can have confidence we're praying according to God's will. We expect Him to grant us, in His own timing, these qualities of the Christian life we're seeking. But I think that subconsciously we must believe that God answers them with a kind of supernatural lightning bolt. Something like, "Well, bless your heart, child, here's all the faith, love, and Christ-likeness you'll ever need." Zap!

Well, guess what—it doesn't usually work that way.

Do you want to mature in your Christian walk? Then expect some suffering.

> Not only so, but we also rejoice in our sufferings, because we know that *suffering produces perseverance*; perseverance, character; and character, hope. And hope does not disappoint us, because God has poured out his love into our hearts by the Holy Spirit, whom he has given us. (Romans 5:3-5)

Do you want to have your faith strengthened? Then expect your faith to be tested.

> Consider it pure joy, my brothers, whenever you face trials of many kinds, because you know that the *testing of your faith* develops perseverance. Perseverance must finish its work *so that you may be mature* and complete, not lacking anything. (James 1:2-4)

Do you want God to use you to minister to others? Then expect God to first comfort you during your own pain.

> Praise be to the God and Father of our Lord Jesus Christ, the Father of compassion and the God of all comfort, who comforts us in all *our troubles, so that we can comfort* those in any trouble with the comfort we ourselves have received from God. (2 Corinthians 1:3-4)

Do you want to know God better? Then expect to give up the things of this world that are holding you back.

> But whatever was to my profit I now consider loss for the sake of Christ. What is more, I consider everything a loss compared to the surpassing greatness of *knowing Christ Jesus my Lord, for whose sake I have lost all things*. I consider them rubbish, so that I may gain Christ and be found in him. . . . I want to know Christ and the power of his resurrection and the fellowship of sharing in his sufferings. (Philippians 3:7-10)

Do you want to glorify Him with your life? Then expect to go through trials.

> In this you greatly rejoice, though now for a little while you may have had to suffer grief in *all kinds of trials*.

These have come so that your faith—of greater worth than gold, which perishes even though refined by fire—may be proved genuine and *may result in praise, glory and honor* when Jesus Christ is revealed. (1 Peter 1:6-7)

Most Christians, at one time or another, will ask God why He allows pain, suffering, and disappointment...

...to touch His children (in general) and touch *us* (in particular). When we meet the Lord face to face, we'll have an opportunity to ask Him in person (although seeing His glory may be all the answer we need). I wouldn't be surprised if part of the answer turns out to be: "Those things happened *because I was answering your prayers, in order to give you what you asked for.*"

As I began to gain an insight into this, I found myself uplifted. Trials are all the more difficult if they seem to be needless or a waste. Once you begin to see that they are purposeful, it's a great thing because then you know that (1) they will come to an end when the purpose is accomplished, (2) you will somehow, in some way, have gained something of great value, and (3) you will have glorified God by trusting Him and giving Him time to work.

A passage that was very encouraging to me during this time was Jeremiah 29:10-14. God is revealing to the Israelites why they are having the excruciating experience of being taken as slaves into the Babylonian captivity.

> [10]This is what the Lord says: "When seventy years are completed for Babylon, I will come to you and fulfill my gracious promise to bring you back to this place. [11]For I know the plans I have for you," declares the Lord, "plans to prosper you and not to harm you, plans to give you hope and a future. [12]Then you will call upon me, and come and pray to me, and I will listen to you. [13]You will seek me and find me when you seek me with all your heart. [14]I will be found by you," declares the Lord, "and will bring you back from captivity."

Here are the encouraging truths I found in this passage:

▶ Trials eventually come to an end, and God can be absolutely counted upon to fulfill His promises (verse 10).

▶ God is still thinking about us, even when we're feeling lonely in our trials (verse 11). He is listening to our heartfelt prayers (verse 12).

▶ The only thoughts that God has toward us are thoughts that include a future that is hopeful and good (verse 11).

▶ God allows our trials to come because they are necessary to accomplish His purpose in our lives (verse 11).

▶ God's purpose is that we would seek Him (verse 13).

▶ God allows Himself to be found when we search for Him with all our heart. He purposes to ultimately bring about our restoration (verses 13-14).

In this passage, the Israelites have been removed from their land and torn from their possessions, yet God does not tell them to seek the restoration of their land. He does not tell them to seek their possessions. He does not tell them to seek their freedom. He tells them to seek but one thing—Himself. And one way that God has of causing us to seek Him whole-heartedly is by allowing us to lose those other things that we highly prize.

As I sought the Lord during those days, I opened my mind and heart to whatever He had purposed for me. I had previously assumed I would continue in the investment advisory profession for the remainder of my career; now I wasn't so sure. Perhaps the Lord was using these difficult circumstances to change the direction of my working life. As long as I was financially comfortable and had a large client base, why would I consider anything else?

So, just in case this was part of the agenda (when you're seeking God's leading, you pray a lot of "just in case" prayers), I surrendered to the Lord all aspects of my professional life. If He wanted to rebuild my company, that would be fine. If He wanted me to take a job working for someone else, that would be fine. If He wanted me to leave the business world and go back into full-time ministry work, that would be fine. I was finally in the best place for a child of God to be: "Whatever You want, Lord, before You even reveal it, the answer is yes."

I added a little P.S. "If You think it would be OK, I'd like work that's mentally challenging, emotionally satisfying, and which somehow involves a ministry to people." Through a series of incidents (which I explain in chapter 36 of *Sound Mind Investing*), the Lord led me to begin a new career in writing and publishing. One of the great blessings of my new work has been the number of warm and encouraging letters I receive from my readers. They express appreciation for the fact they are understanding certain financial and investing matters for the first time, and the new hope they have that they can really take control of their investment lives rather than relying on others. Their enthusiasm, and the number of them that say my monthly newsletter "is an answer to prayer," is quite humbling. I never expected to feel such a sense of personal kinship with so many people I've never met.

I mention this only to point out how wonderfully God answered my prayer that He would give me a ministry as well as a business. He has, and I've never felt so gratified by anything I've done in my professional life.

Investing that glorifies God enjoys His blessings.

As I indicated at the beginning of this section, it's a tricky matter to accurately discern how certain experiences in life will ultimately work for our good. The reason for this is not that bad things are necessarily good things in disguise, but rather our God is so great that He can take the bad things and *transform* them into good things. He does this because He purposes to use everything in life that we might "be conformed to the likeness of his Son." Knowing that what appears good (wealth and success) can actually be bad for us, and that what appears bad ("trials of many kinds") can actually be good for us, gives one a certain humility in praying.

This truth is beautifully expressed in the *Prayer of an Unknown Confederate Soldier*:

I asked God for strength that I might achieve.

I was made weak, that I might learn humbly to obey.

I asked for help, that I might do greater things.

I was given infirmity, that I might do better things.

I asked for riches, that I might be happy.

I was given poverty, that I might be wise.

I asked for power, that I might have the praise of men.

I was given weakness, that I might feel the need of God.

I asked for all things, that I might enjoy life.

I was given life, that I might enjoy all things.

I got nothing that I asked for but everything I hoped for.

Almost despite myself, my unspoken prayers were answered.

I am, among all men, most richly blessed.

(Source Unknown)

We're all looking for peace in an uncertain world. We don't know what the future holds, but we know who holds the future. Our trust in Him is never misplaced. Paul wrote: "For me, to live is Christ, and to die is gain." *Paul* could say that because dying brought him even more of what he was living for. But today, if for us "to live is business success," then to die is loss. If for us "to live is financial riches," then to die is loss. If for us "to live is the praise of men," then to die is loss. Because dying takes all of those things away. On the day that we die, what wealth we may have will be of zero value to us, of no help or comfort whatsoever. But knowing Him will mean everything. And that's why He is our peace.

If you'll aim your life in the direction of God's glory, you'll enjoy His blessings. They may or may not be material blessings. But in whatever form God sends them, you can be sure they will satisfy your deepest longings. "Praise be to the God and Father of our Lord Jesus Christ, who has blessed us in the heavenly realms with every spiritual blessing in Christ" (Ephesians 1:3). ◆

Sound Mind Investing
THE FINANCIAL JOURNAL FOR TODAY'S CHRISTIAN FAMILY

Dear Valued Reader:

I hope this booklet has been helpful to you. If so, I believe you'd enjoy reading through a complimentary issue of my monthly *Sound Mind Investing* financial newsletter. It's based on biblically-based values and priorities (see pages 4-5), and gives you:

Help in setting and achieving realistic, personalized goals. You'll find no claims that I can predict coming economic events or market turns. Mine is a slow-but-sure, conservative strategy that emphasizes controlling your risk according to your age, goals, and personal investing temperament.

Very specific, timely advice. I recommend specific no-load mutual funds. For each of four different risk categories, I not only tell you *what to buy* and *how much to buy*, but just as importantly, *when to sell and buy something else!*

Monthly "economic earthquake" updates. I include an economic primer that will help you understand the implications of the unfolding economic tremors. Plus, there are data and graphs of various economic indicators that will be especially helpful in giving us fair warning if a crisis seems to be approaching.

I'd like you to have the opportunity to see these benefits for yourself. Send in the attached postage-paid card for your free issue — there's absolutely no obligation to subscribe. I hope to hear from you soon!

Free!
A Sample Issue of
Sound Mind Investing

□ Yes, send my free issue!

Austin: I'm taking you up on your offer of a complimentary sample of your monthly *Sound Mind Investing* newsletter. Please send my free issue and subscription information to me at the address below.

Name: _____

Address: _____

City: _____

State: _____ Zip: _____

Free!
A Sample Issue of
Sound Mind Investing